300 500 229 C0

THE YELLOW RIVER

written and photographed by

Julia Waterlow

Wayland

THE WORLD'S RIVERS

The Amazon
The Danube
The Ganges
The Mississippi
The Nile
The Rhine
The Seine
The Thames
The Volga
The Yellow River

Cover *The Yellow River passes through the mountains and valleys of the Tibetan Plateau picking up soil and silt.*

Series editor Rosemary Ashley
Series designer Derek Lee
Editorial and design Paul Bennett

First published in 1993 by
Wayland (Publishers) Limited
61 Western Road, Hove
East Sussex, BN3 1JD, England

British Library Cataloguing in Publication Data
Waterlow, Julia
Yellow River.—(World's Rivers Series)
I. Title   II. Series
915.11

ISBN 0-7502-0772-8

Typeset in the UK by
Dorchester Typesetting Group Ltd
Printed in Italy by G. Canale C.S.p.A.

CONTENTS

1. CHINA'S SORROW

For more than 5,000 years people have made their homes beside the great river of northern China, the Yellow River. It was here that the first Chinese towns and cities grew and the early emperors held court; because of this, the area through which the river flows is often called the cradle of Chinese civilization. Although not quite the longest river in China, the Yellow River is the most important in the country's history.

The Yellow River gets its name from the yellowish-grey soil that it picks up along its course, and by the time it reaches the plains of north China it is rather like a thick soup. The Yellow River is one of the muddiest rivers in the world: the Chinese say that if you fall into it, you will never get clean again.

Although it has always provided rich soil and plenty of water for farming, the Yellow River has burst its banks many times. Streaming in terrible floods across huge areas of northern China, the river has caused millions of people to die. So it has been nicknamed 'China's Sorrow'.

From nomads roaming the cold mountain wastes and deserts, to farming communities and industrial cities in the fertile plains of north China, the river passes almost the whole range of Chinese life. In order to make living here at all possible, the Yellow River has had to be controlled. For centuries work to deepen, contain and divert the river has been necessary, both to contain the floods and to provide water to irrigate the land.

The Yellow River winds through the desert in the western province of Ningxia.

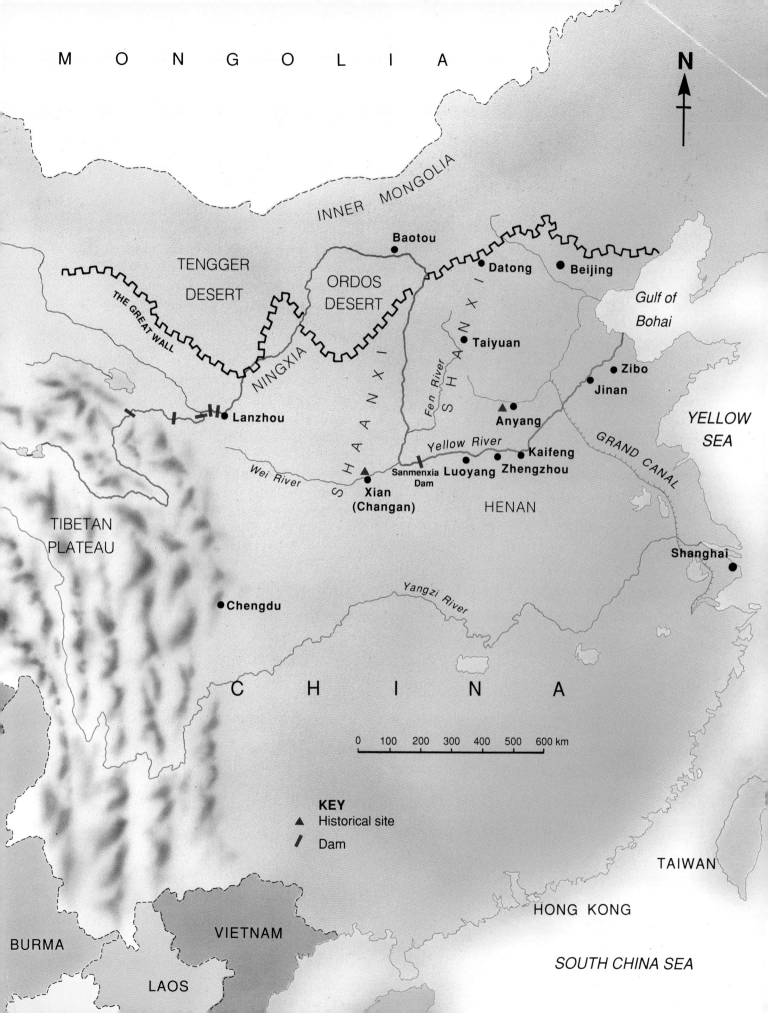

2. THE COURSE OF THE YELLOW RIVER

The roof of the world

The Tibetan Plateau forms most of western China. It is an upland area slashed by a series of mountain ranges. Because of the great height of the region – an average of 3,000 metres above sea level – it is often called the 'roof of the world'. Many of Asia's great rivers rise here, including the Yellow River.

From a spring that surfaces at an altitude of about 4,300 metres, a small stream that will later become the Yellow River trickles across a wide basin on the plateau. It flows east, crossing an area dotted with lakes, known as the Sea of Stars. The countryside is wild and barren, covered only with rough grass. The climate is so harsh that in winter the bitter cold freezes the streams.

The growing river twists and bends through small irrigated plains and then through narrow rocky valleys. It remains shallow and fast-flowing, widening as tributaries add their water to it. More than 1,500 kilometres later, it reaches the edge of the Tibetan Plateau and pours out through gorges, several of which have been dammed, to flatter lands around Lanzhou.

Left *High on the bleak Tibetan Plateau, the landscape is dotted with yaks grazing on the thin grass.*

Right *The Liujiaxia reservoir near Lanzhou where the Yellow River has been dammed.*

The Great Wall
Stretching across northern China like a long noodle, the Great Wall was designed to keep out invaders from the north. It had 25,000 forts and watch-towers along its length of nearly 4,000 kilometres. Started in about 200 BC, different sections have been built at different times over the centuries. In places deserts have taken over and dunes nearly cover the remains of the wall.

The Great Bend

East of Lanzhou the Yellow River turns north. In a huge loop, it flows up through Ningxia Province and into Inner Mongolia before heading south again. This region is very dry, much of it with less than 250 mm of rain per year. Deserts lie all around and it is only because of the waters of the Yellow River that people can live and farm here.

At the top of the great bend, in Inner Mongolia, mountains border the river to the north and beyond lie rich grasslands. To the south is the Ordos Desert. This area used to lie outside the Chinese empire and was occupied by people that the Chinese called 'barbarians'. To keep them out, the Great Wall was built,

stretching nearly 4,000 kilometres across northern China. The remains of the Great Wall cross this part of the Yellow River and snake along the south of the Ordos Desert.

The sandy deserts that surround the Yellow River are blown continually by winds from the north and east. The sand is shifting closer to occupied areas, and in places has covered roads, railways and farmland. In the Ordos Desert, hundreds of kilometres of trees have been planted to stabilize the sand and form a barrier. Roughly following the line of the Great Wall, this belt of trees is sometimes called the 'Great Green Wall'. In other areas the sand has been controlled by mats of straw laid across the dunes, which hold the sand in place.

The Yellow River is used for irrigating the fields as it flows through flatter lands around Lanzhou.

Straw mats hold sand dunes in place beside the Yellow River. Small shrubs are able to grow, stabilizing the sand.

Across the relatively flat plains of Ningxia and Inner Mongolia, the river is broad and shallow. Due to the lack of rain, there are virtually no tributaries along this stretch of the river. But where it turns south again, the river enters another hilly area, known as the loess region, and many smaller rivers join it.

Loess

This region, on the borders of Shanxi and Shaanxi provinces, is where the Yellow River becomes truly yellow and laden with mud. The whole area is covered in loess. This is a type of fine, yellowish soil that feels rather like talcum powder.

A large area of northern China is covered by loess soil.

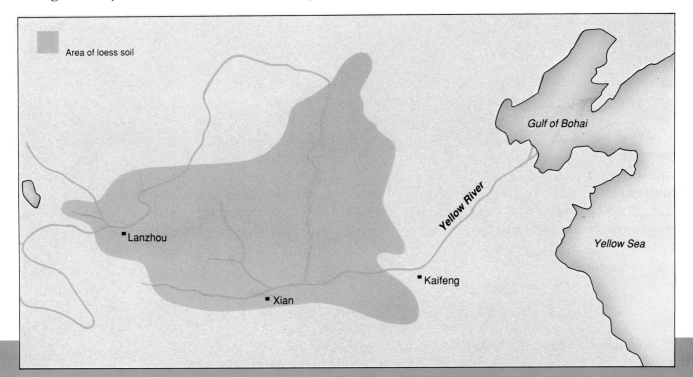

Area of loess soil

Lanzhou

Yellow River

Gulf of Bohai

Yellow Sea

Kaifeng

Xian

Loess scenery. The loess soil is heavily eroded, forming steep gullies. Fields perch on top.

Over thousands of years particles of earth have been blown from the deserts in the north-west and have built up a thick blanket of loess.

The rainfall is also low here (less than 500 mm per year) and most of it falls in summer in heavy downpours. The fine loess is easily washed away, especially since there is little tree cover. Deep gullies are left and landslides can crash down the hillsides, causing many valleys to become steep, sheer-sided ravines. The river and its tributaries pick up vast amounts of loess and carry it downstream. Although it has already picked up some loess at other points upstream, the river collects 90 per cent of its total load of soil here.

The river flows through the loess area in a series of impassable gorges which are surrounded by dry, dusty hills.

The landscape is mostly bare of trees and everything seems the same dull yellow colour. As in much of north China, winters are bitterly cold, spring brings dusty winds and summers are hot. The rainfall is unreliable, sometimes leading to drought.

Two major tributaries enter the Yellow River here: the Wei and the Fen. Both rivers have flat valleys with good soil which provided two of the earliest farmed areas in China, and they remain important agricultural areas today. Soon after these tributaries join the Yellow River, it turns sharply to the east and cuts its way through the surrounding hills in more gorges. A huge dam, called Sanmenxia, holds back the waters in a long reservoir. Beyond the dam, the river finally flows out on to the North China Plain.

The North China Plain

This enormous plain is almost at sea level, so the Yellow River slows right down and begins dropping its massive load of silt. Over the ages, the deposited sediment has built up and up, raising the level of the river bed until, like a shining road, the river flows between 3 and 4 metres above the level of the plain. In places it lies 10 metres above the land! Because it is raised so high, along the last 800 kilometres or so across the plain, no more tributaries are able to join the Yellow River.

Beside the river, the deposited material forms natural banks, called levees or dykes; these have been reinforced, widened and built up by people over the centuries. The distance between the dykes on either side of the river can be vast – at Kaifeng, for example, they are 13 kilometres apart.

In the winter, the dry season, the Yellow River often only fills a small part of its wide, shallow bed. However, during the summer the river can swell to a hundred times its winter size. It is common in the north of China for rain to fall suddenly and heavily. In the past, the dykes did not always hold the sudden rush of water; they gave way and the river flooded the surrounding countryside.

A cross-section of the Yellow River as it crosses the North China Plain.

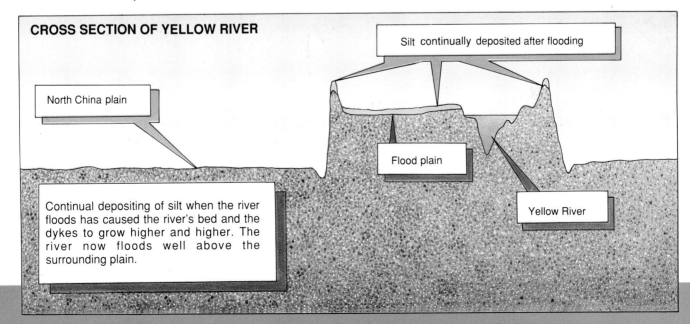

CROSS SECTION OF YELLOW RIVER

Silt continually deposited after flooding

North China plain

Flood plain

Yellow River

Continual depositing of silt when the river floods has caused the river's bed and the dykes to grow higher and higher. The river now floods well above the surrounding plain.

10

The Yellow River crosses the North China Plain near Kaifeng. Large amounts of silt have been deposited beside the water.

Rich river soil covers the North China Plain and it is one of the main farming regions of China, where millions of people live. Today their lives are safeguarded from flooding and drought by careful control of the river. Pumping stations are dotted along its banks and its water is used for irrigation.

The Yellow River dykes on the North China Plain are wide enough to take a road along the top.

The river finally reaches the sea 5,464 kilometres from its source. Its delta is shallow, marshy and salty and it is difficult to tell which is land and which is water. It is here that the river drops its remaining load of silt. Millions of years ago, where the North China Plain is today, this area was covered by sea; the plain was formed by the deposited silt of the Yellow River. The plain continues to grow at a very fast rate. For example, between 1949 and 1951 the coast at the mouth of the Yellow River grew further into the sea by about 10 kilometres.

Facts and figures
Length: 5,464 km.
Number of major tributaries: about 40.
Height at source: 4,300 m.
Area of river basin: 750,000 sq km.
Amount of silt carried: 1.6 billion tonnes of loess downstream every year, half goes into the sea and half is dropped en route.
There are 9 large hydroelectric power projects on the river, 174 large and medium reservoirs in the valley, and 80 hydroelectric power stations in all.
The Yellow River basin has 40 per cent of the total water of northern China.

3. THE CRADLE OF CHINESE CIVILIZATION

Early settlement

China has the longest continuous civilization of any country in the world. The oldest evidence of humans in China is the 600,000-year-old fossil remains of the cave-dwelling 'Peking Man', found near Beijing. Organized society in China is believed to have started in the Yellow River valley. Archaeologists have found signs of farming and settled communities dating back 6,000 years.

The area where the Yellow River enters the North China Plain was home to all China's early dynasties. It was a fertile region, well-protected by surrounding hills and above the regular flooding of the plain. We know little about the two earliest dynasties, the Xia and Shang, whose kingdoms lasted

Dynasties and governments

2300–1700 BC	Xia
1700–1100	Shang
1100–221	Zhou and Warring States
221–207	Qin
207 BC–AD 220	Han
AD 581–618	Sui
618–907	Tang
960–1279	Song
1279–1368	Yuan (Mongolians)
1368–1644	Ming
1644–1911	Qing
1912–1949	Chinese Republic
1949–now	People's Republic of China

from about 2000 to 1000 BC. But the remains of early cities have been found – at Anyang, the last Shang capital, animal bones with writing scratched on them were discovered, for example.

A model of a 6,000-year-old neolithic house in the Wei River valley. These houses were built half underground.

Cheng Weimin

'I work as a photographer at the Yellow River Park near Zhengzhou. This is a special park built beside the river, with trees, temples and places for viewing the Yellow River. Many people come to have their picture taken in front of the statue of mother and child which you can see behind me. The mother represents the Yellow River and the baby represents China. We call the Yellow River the cradle of Chinese civilization because it was in this area more than 6,000 years ago that the first Chinese people started farming the land.'

These are probably the origin of the characters used today by the Chinese in their writing.

Over the next 800 years individual states sprang up and the civilized area spread further. Despite wars and power struggles, art and learning flourished. In 221 BC these kingdoms were united into one country, China, under the Qin emperor. His capital was near the present-day city of Xian on the Wei River.

Canals like this one in Ningxia were built as long as 2,000 years ago to irrigate the land.

China expands

The Qin emperor was a cruel but strong leader. He created a common writing system, standardized weights and measures and began the building of the Great Wall. The emperor's powerful control of his people meant that he was able to force huge numbers of men and women to build major public works. In order to provide irrigation and so increase the amount of food that could be produced for his expanding empire, he organized the building of canals both in the Yellow River valley and elsewhere.

Canals were useful because only short stretches of the Yellow River were navigable by boat. In the following Han dynasty, to provide easy transport of goods from the North China Plain to the Wei valley, a long canal was built to the south bypassing the river's gorges. While providing irrigation for farmland, its most important use was to bring grain to the capital. The emperor demanded a 'grain tribute'. Grain had to be sent regularly to the capital to feed him, his court, and the army, and also to be kept as a store for times of famine.

In about AD 220, 'barbarians' from the north invaded and China split into several kingdoms again. The newcomers, too, made their capital near the Yellow River at Luoyang. Here, Buddhism,

Buddhist statues carved out of the cliffs near Luoyang date back to about AD 500.

a relatively new religion to China, flourished. Four hundred years later, under the Tang dynasty, China was united again and reached a high point of civilization. As many dynasties had done before them, they built their capital, Changan (now Xian), in the Wei valley.

At the time of the Tang dynasty, Changan was probably the greatest city in the world. About one million people lived inside its walls and another million outside. It was a rich city, having highly developed culture and arts as well as being a thriving commercial centre. Merchants were drawn in from all over China as canals, roads and inns were built, improving transport links to the city. From the sea ports and along caravan routes, such as the Silk Road, people arrived from all over the world bringing new religions and ideas.

The highly organized Tang system of government and its capital city began to decline in about AD 900. The following Song dynasty established their capital at Kaifeng, but when in 1211 the

Called the Big Wild Goose Pagoda, this beautiful building was built in AD 648.

Terracotta army
Before the Qin emperor died (in 210 BC), he had 750,000 men working to build him a tomb. Sculptors created a life-size army out of clay, soldiers, horses and chariots to guard the emperor in the afterlife. The workers were buried with the secret of the emperor's tomb, and it was only this century that this magnificent army was discovered.

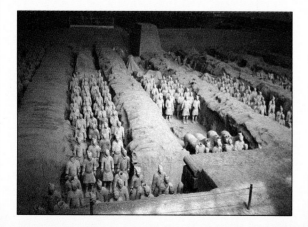

Mongolian armies of the warrior king Genghis Khan began to sweep over the Great Wall, the Song people were pushed south and their city was destroyed.

The Yellow River valley was never home to China's government again. The Mongolians made Beijing their capital and it has remained China's capital almost ever since. Although the centre of power may no longer lie in the valley of the Yellow River, it remains a fertile agricultural region and an important source of water for all north China.

The Grand Canal

China is home to the longest human-made canal in the world: the Grand Canal. When its full length was completed in 1290, it stretched about 1,100 kilometres from the Yangzi River, crossing the Yellow River and finally ending in Beijing. It was designed to provide transport, mainly of grain, to the capital from the rich farming areas of the Yangzi.

The emperor's palace, called the Forbidden City, in Beijing.

4. CHINA TODAY

Land and people

China is the third largest country in the world. However, only about one-third of this vast area is suitable for farming and settlement. Much of the western half is high mountains or desert. The flatter, good farming land is mostly in the east, so this is where the Chinese have traditionally settled. Today it is the most heavily populated part of China.

The north has extremes of temperature and uncertain rainfall, but south of the Yangzi River, the climate gradually becomes more tropical. It gets warmer and wetter all year round and it is here that most of China's rice is grown.

Over a billion people live in China, more than a fifth of all the people in the world. About three-quarters of them still work on the land as farmers, but China has a huge industrialization programme and the cities are growing fast. The speed at which the population is increasing has caused great concern and so in 1979 the government passed a law which forbade families to have more than one child (the policy was known as 'one couple, one child'). Even so, the population continues to grow by several millions every year.

In China, families are forbidden to have more than one child.

Wu Suxian

'I am a bus driver. Nowadays, many girls in China drive buses. I work on bus number 5, in the city of Sanmenxia which lies beside the Yellow River. Like everyone in China, I work six days a week. My day off is Wednesday. Every morning I get up at 5 o'clock to get to work in time to drive the first bus. It starts just after 6 o'clock, and is crowded with people going to work at the factories in Sanmenxia. The bus I drive has two bus conductresses who not only collect tickets from the passengers, but also help me to fix the bus when it breaks down.'

Attitudes and politics

In Chinese, China means 'Middle Kingdom'. The mountains to the west and the sea to the south and east have kept China remote. The Chinese have always thought of their country as being the centre of the civilized world and have not felt a great need to explore or make contact with other countries. However, since the 1980s, the Chinese government has been cautiously allowing foreign ideas and influences into the country.

The ruling political party in China is the Communist Party. Since the party came to power in 1949, life for many Chinese families, particularly in the countryside, has improved a great deal. Most people now have enough to eat, a roof over their heads and young people can generally read and write. However, life is restricted compared with other countries. Usually people have little choice about what work they can do or

Early in the morning, two men sit listening to their caged birds singing.

Public information is given on posters like this one about traffic safety.

where they can live. Often they belong to a 'work unit' which provides their job, housing, schools, medical care and recreational facilities. This system is called the 'iron rice bowl' (meaning an unbreakable rice bowl) in China because everyone is guaranteed a job, and so food, for life.

Since the beginning of the 1980s, there has been more freedom to start private businesses, for farmers to sell their extra produce on the open market and for business people to trade with foreigners. The Chinese are keen business people and, in the last few years, private enterprise has blossomed. China's economy is now one of the fastest growing in the world.

5. PEOPLE OF THE YELLOW RIVER

Most of China's people are of Chinese origin; they are called Han Chinese. The remaining 100 million or so are a mixture of different peoples who originally came from other countries or whose lands had been conquered and settled by the Chinese. Although along the lower reaches of the Yellow River the majority of the population is Han Chinese, further upstream live three different types of people: Tibetans, Muslims and Mongolians.

Tibetans

Tibetans live high on the plateau where the Yellow River rises. Their country once extended across the whole upland area of western China and into the valleys at the edges, but China now rules Tibet. Tibetans are a different race from the Chinese, traditionally living from simple farming, such as growing barley and other hardy grains, and herding yaks and sheep. Many were and still are

Many Tibetan people are nomads who live in tents and keep a herd of yaks like these.

21

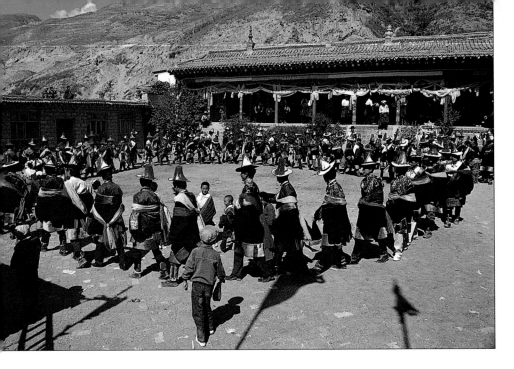

Tibetans have many colourful festivals during the year.

nomads, moving with their tents in the summer to higher pastures for fresh grazing. Much of the land is bleak and remote with few roads, so travel is difficult.

Tibetans are Buddhists and their religion is a very important part of their lives. As often as they can, Tibetans make pilgrimages to holy temples to make offerings and pray. Their houses contain religious pictures and outside they may have a prayer flag. This is a special flag with prayers written on it – they believe that when it flutters in the wind the prayers will blow to the gods.

Muslims

The Muslims are one of the biggest minority groups in China and most live in the north-west of the country. Hundreds of years ago Arab traders came along the Silk Road and a few remained in China. Some Chinese Muslims are their descendants and others are Chinese who were converted to the Muslim religion, Islam. Most Muslims who live in the Yellow River area (mainly near Lanzhou and in Ningxia Province) have adopted a Chinese way of life, but many also

Bai Shangjun

'My home is in a town on the Yellow River near Lanzhou where many Muslim people live. I am of a different race from the Chinese, called the Salar. Several centuries ago, my ancestors fled from a cruel leader called Tamerlane who ruled countries to the west of China. They trekked with camels until they found a place to stop which reminded them of their homeland. Here they settled. Over the years Salars have kept their Muslim religion and old traditions. There are about a million of us now in China.'

People stop to eat lamb kebabs cooked by a Muslim man at a street stall in the city of Lanzhou.

still proudly follow their traditions and religion.

The Muslims often wear similar clothes to the Chinese, but some have quite European faces. Men sometimes wear a white cap and have beards (few Chinese have beards) and some groups of Muslim women cover their heads.

Scattered around the Muslim towns and cities are mosques and at prayer time the priest, or imam, calls the people to prayer. After centuries of living with the Chinese and because of persecution, the Muslims no longer observe their religious practices strictly. However, like Muslims all over the world, they do not eat pork.

Mongolians

Where the Yellow River reaches its most northerly point on the great bend, it flows through another area where non-Chinese people live. This area is called Inner Mongolia. To the north of the Chinese border lies Mongolia (formerly Outer Mongolia), a huge country which was part of the Soviet Union for many years but is now an independent state. In the days of Ghengis Khan and his sons (between about AD 1200 and AD 1350), the Mongolian empire stretched for thousands of kilometres. It included China and reached to the edges of Europe. It was the largest empire the world has ever known.

Much of Mongolia (both Inner and 'Outer') is grassland and the Mongolians have always been great herdsmen, keeping sheep, horses, goats, cattle and camels. Their skilful horsemanship was one of the reasons they were able to conquer seemingly strong countries such as China so easily. Traditionally nomads, some Mongolians still live in 'yurts', which are round tents made of felt that they can take with them as they move from pasture to pasture.

Today, most Mongolians have settled in houses on the grasslands and breed sheep. Not many of the traditional Mongolian customs remain here in China and only a few people still follow the traditional Buddhist religion. However, in summer, there are still large fairs where the Mongolians put on horse races and take part in wrestling matches.

Sheep and goats are grazed on the huge open grasslands of Mongolia.

A Tibetan places an offering in a Buddhist temple. Religion plays an important part in the lives of Tibetan people.

The Cultural Revolution

The Communists who came to power in China in 1949 were against religion. This situation came to a head during the Cultural Revolution (1966–76), a time of great upheaval when people were told to get rid of all their old ideas and only think about building a modern socialist state. Minorities, such as the Tibetans, Muslims and Mongolians, suffered more than most. Monasteries, mosques and temples were destroyed and monks and priests were killed.

China's present government is now allowing a little religious freedom; places of worship are being rebuilt and people are permitted to go to them to pray.

6. INDUSTRY AND CITIES

Natural resources

Underneath the yellow blanket of loess in the area around the Yellow River, lies China's most important natural resource: coal. Coal is used in China both by industry and at home for cooking and heating. To the east of the Yellow River in the province of Shanxi lies about one-third of China's total coal reserves, the biggest mines being near the cities of Datong and Taiyuan. It is known that there are still huge untapped reserves in many parts of the Yellow River basin.

The Yellow River area is rich in other minerals too, such as iron ore, bauxite and copper. Near the mouth of the river at Shenli, oil was found and there is now a large refinery. In the mountainous area towards the source of the river, the Chinese believe that there may also be rich deposits of valuable minerals.

Cities have grown where minerals have been discovered but many of the Yellow River's cities were already large or important. For example, the city of Lanzhou has always been a great trading centre, because in the old days it was the last city in China on the Silk Road – beyond it lay barbarians and deserts.

Sand and gravel are dug out of the bed of a Yellow River tributary. They are used for building.

Right *The Yellow River flows through the middle of the city of Lanzhou.*

Lanzhou

Ponies and camels used to amble down the streets of Lanzhou, but it is now a huge modern city of 1.5 million people, and the main industrial centre in north-west China. Two things made it grow quickly: the discovery of oil to the north-west in the early 1950s, and the arrival of the railway in 1960, linking the city to the rest of China. Today Lanzhou stretches some 40 kilometres along the banks of the Yellow River, the huge oil refinery and chemical factories belching out smoke over busy streets.

With such a concentration of industry there is pollution. The air in many parts of the city is thick with the smell of chemicals. The Yellow River is suffering from waste products being poured into it, too. There used to be eighteen different kinds of fish here but eight are now extinct. The Chinese argue that because they are still a developing country they are too poor to afford expensive pollution controls.

Chinese cities are crowded with bicycles, which are used instead of cars. This bicycle park is in Kaifeng.

The walls of the ancient city of Xian. All Chinese cities used to be built with walls around them for defence against attack from enemies .

Baotou and Xian

Downstream in Inner Mongolia lies the city of Baotou, the northernmost city on the Yellow River. Before the Communists came to power it was of little importance, but when both iron and coal were found in the region and the railway lines improved in the early 1950s, it grew rapidly. Now it has one of China's biggest iron and steel factories. The Mongolians who live and work there are now a minority in their own city – most of the population are Han Chinese brought in to work in the new factories.

To the south, in the Wei River valley, many great cities rose during the early Chinese dynasties. The valley was at the centre of China's main agricultural region and was also an area that could be easily defended from attack. When other parts of China became more important, the area declined, but the city of Xian remained. Xian's growth this century into a modern city of nearly 2.5 million people was due to the Communists' industrial programme and the building of rail links.

Left *There are many small industries in China, like this one near Baotou which smelts and recycles unwanted metal.*

Right *A coal-fired power station in Ningxia. The Yellow River area is rich in coal, one of China's most valuable resources.*

Cities of the North China Plain

Downstream, on the banks of the Yellow River itself, are the towns of Luoyang, Zhengzhou and Kaifeng. All three can claim to have once been the capital of China. Zhengzhou was the earliest, the capital nearly 4,000 years ago. In the 1950s a brand new city was built at Zhengzhou. It is the capital of Henan Province (Henan means 'south of the river') and is a major industrial centre for the region.

Nearby, Luoyang, which has been China's capital on several occasions, is one of the richest historical sites in China. Today the huge new industrial city beside the older part is well known for the tractors and other agricultural machinery it produces. Kaifeng too was once a capital of China for a short time. Unlike Zhengzhou and Luoyang, which have populations of around a million people, Kaifeng has not seen so much modernization and today remains a small town.

The provincial capital of Jinan was once famous for its silk and it grew with the arrival of a railway in 1904. During this period foreign countries, such as Germany, England and Japan, were establishing trading areas and building factories in China, particularly in towns near the coast. Not far away, at Zibo, the discovery of coal has led to this town growing into a major industrial area of over 2 million people in the last twenty years.

Some of the buildings in Kaifeng which have been rebuilt in the old Song dynasty style.

7. LIFE IN THE COUNTRYSIDE

The North China Plain

Across the flat North China Plain lie thousands of villages of mud-brick houses surrounded by fields of wheat. Because of the cold, dry climate, rice is not easily grown; so wheat is the main crop and noodles the staple food. Beside the villages are vegetable plots, fruit orchards and fish ponds where carp are raised. In the walled courtyards of many of the houses, there are chickens and pigs.

The soil is rich from the silt deposited by the river over the centuries, though fertilizers are now needed to produce a good crop. Cotton, millet, kaoliang (a grain) and soya beans can be grown in the summer as well as wheat and barley. With the huge Chinese population to feed, previously unused land by the coast is being reclaimed for farming. The soil of the reclaimed land contains sea salts and plants cannot grow in it. River water is flushed through the sand to clean out the salts before crops can be grown.

Farmers spread their wheat on the road so that the passing vehicles thresh it for them.

31

In most areas near the Yellow River, farmers use animals for ploughing.

For nearly all the people who live on the land in north China, life is hard, not only because much of the farm work is still done by hand, but also because of the climate. As well as the bitterly cold winters, the unreliable rainfall means a continual effort to build channels to irrigate the fields. The Yellow River provides the only certain source of water for many people living along its course.

Desert and mountain life

Ningxia Province is particularly dependent on the Yellow River. Canals were first built 2,000 years ago to irrigate this desert-like region and today a green fertile strip of farmland lies on both sides of the river. As well as wheat, the short but hot summer season allows fruits such as peaches and melons to be

Li Yangguan

'I am a shepherd in the Yin Shan mountains, just north of the Yellow River in Inner Mongolia. My family has about a hundred sheep which I take out all day, every day, to graze in the hills. We also keep some goats. We have both kinds of animals for their wool, though we do eat their meat too. See the stone I have put on my forked stick? This is to control my sheep. When I throw the stone with the stick, I can make the stone fly a long way to scare the sheep in whatever direction I want them to go.'

Planting out rice seedlings during the short summer season. The Yellow River provides the water that rice needs in order to grow.

cultivated, and fields of yellow sunflowers, grown for their seeds, stretch to the edge of the watered area. With its abundance of water from the maze of irrigation canals, the area supports a crop of summer rice each year. People keep animals too, with sheep being more common than pigs because of the Muslim influence.

In the mountainous area where the river rises, the main farming activity is raising animals such as yaks and sheep. Where there are sheltered valleys, barley, maize, potatoes and some fruits are grown. Along much of the upper part of the Yellow River oil-seed rape and flax are grown, which are used mainly to make oils for cooking.

Houses

All along the Yellow River valley, houses in the countryside are built of mud bricks, made from the fine loess soil. Most are single-storey buildings with just one or two rooms. Inside there is a wide brick platform which is heated from below by a fire. Called 'kangs', these platforms are covered in rugs and used as beds or sitting places, and the fires keep the houses warm through the winter.

Few people in the country have running water in their houses; most fetch it in buckets from a river or stream, or they rely on wells. For heating and cooking, most people use coal. Not everyone has electricity, but in remote areas it is not uncommon to find schemes that use small rivers to produce electricity for the nearby villages. In some areas the power of the wind is used to produce electricity.

In the loess region in Shaanxi and Shanxi provinces, many of the houses have been built into the sides of cliffs. The soil is soft and easily worked and these cave houses keep warm in the winter and cool in the summer. Living in this area is particularly tough because of the steep hills, the cold winters, droughts and sudden rainstorms that can sweep away roads and fields. Farmers build terraces because this is one of the few ways to grow crops successfully here. Life is easier in the valleys where the land is flatter; farmland can be more easily irrigated and travelling around is not such a problem. The Wei river valley is one of the most productive farming areas in the region, producing both wheat and cotton.

Houses in the loess area around the Yellow River are often built into the soft soil of cliffs.

8. DISASTER AND DIVERSION

Disasters in the past

Although the Yellow River provides good fertile land and water for millions of people, it has flooded more often and killed more people than any other river in the world. Before 1949 it used to flood on average once every two years. Farmers believed it was inhabited by a dragon and made offerings of food and money so that it would not swallow them. At one time girls were sacrificed to keep the 'Lord of the River' happy!

Stories of flooding along the river go back even before records in China began. Legends say that around 2300 BC, massive floods were causing terrible destruction. The emperor appointed a minister, called Yu, to try and tame the river. For thirteen years, without going home to see his family once, Yu worked hard organizing people to deepen the river and build diversion channels to take flood waters. His schemes are said to have made the area safe from floods for hundreds of years.

All the Chinese dynasties were very much concerned with management of the river. There was dredging and dyke building as well as canal construction, both for irrigation and transport. Special government ministries were set up during the Han dynasty (207 BC to AD 220) to deal with the problems of river and water control. It was a continual effort to keep the dykes repaired and the river dredged; if there were political troubles and the organization of the state broke down, the chances were that the dykes would break and there would be a disaster.

Natural disasters often coincided with government collapse and the fall of Chinese dynasties. Floods and droughts were believed to be a sign from heaven that the emperor no longer had the right to rule. In the north of China, a drought lasting from 1877–9 resulted in the death of over 13 million people.

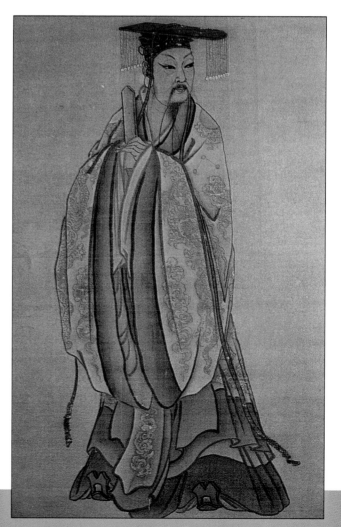

A portrait of Yu the Great, who is said to have tamed the Yellow River over 4,000 years ago.

The Yellow River area also suffered (and continues to suffer) from earthquakes, such as the one in 1920 that resulted in the death of about a quarter of a million people.

In the last 3,000 years the Yellow River has broken its dykes more than 1,500 times and changed its course on twenty-six occasions, nine of which were major diversions. The results were terrible flooding, often lasting for many years.

The costs to the people were enormous: floodwaters ruined farmland, destroyed

Great Yellow River floods	
2297 BC	The first recorded flood (soon after Yu the Great tamed the river). The river flows out to the Gulf of Bohai.
602 BC	The river floods and moves to the south, flowing out to the Yellow Sea.
132 BC	A breach in the dykes of the river remains unrepaired until 109 BC.
29 BC	After a flood, the inhabitants are evacuated. New dykes are built within thirty-six days by dropping stones into the river from boats.
AD 70	The river floods and changes its course to the north, entering the Gulf of Bohai.
AD 923	Dykes are breached as a war tactic to flood enemy territory.
1048	The river moves course further to the north.
1324	It forms a new course far to the south, flowing into the Yellow Sea.
1642	During a peasant revolt, Kaifeng is flooded by breaching the dykes. It is thought that one million people died.
1851	A new course to the north and into the Gulf of Bohai.
1887	After floods, the river turns south along a new 800-kilometre course to link up with the Yangzi River. Over two million people die. Two years later, the river is forced back on its old course, flowing into the Gulf of Bohai.
1898	After floods, up to 3 metres of sand and loess are dumped on surrounding farmland.
1931	Thousands are left homeless after floods.
1933	Three and a half million people are affected by floods.
1938	Chiang Kai Shek breaches the dykes. Nearly one million people die. The river flows south to join with the Yangzi River.
1947	The river returns to its present course.

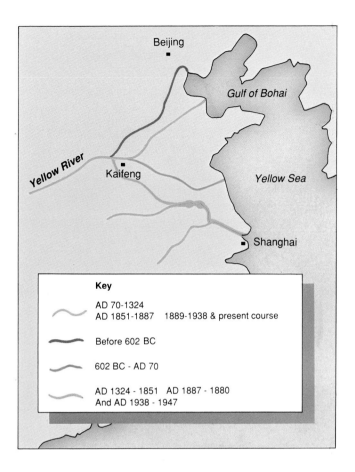

Key

~~	AD 70-1324
	AD 1851-1887 1889-1938 & present course
━━	Before 602 BC
～～	602 BC - AD 70
～～	AD 1324 - 1851 AD 1887 - 1880
	And AD 1938 - 1947

A diagram showing some of the different courses taken by the Yellow River since the seventh century BC.

houses and caused millions of deaths, mostly through the starvation and disease that followed. The effects were felt for years because it was so hard to re-establish crops. Sometimes marshes formed which had to be drained; or there might be thick layers of sand to be cleared. In the same year the flood could well be followed by drought. The scale of most disasters was increased because of the large number of people that lived on the North China Plain.

Chinese women do their washing, safe in the knowledge that the high dykes behind them will keep the Yellow River from flooding.

Changes of course

Where there was a large break in a dyke, the Yellow River not only flooded the land but also took a totally new course. The dykes and the height of the river above the surrounding plain made it almost impossible to redirect the river back on to its original course. Over the years the Yellow River has swung nearly 1,000 kilometres from north to south. For hundreds of years, it flowed to the north of its present course, into the Gulf of Bohai. Severe flooding in the fifth century BC resulted in it taking a route far to the south, flowing out into the Yellow Sea. It has wavered between these two extremes ever since.

It was not always natural causes that created these disasters and made the Yellow River change its course. On several occasions in Chinese history the river has been used as a weapon to defeat an opposing army. One example happened this century.

In 1937 the Japanese invaded China. By 1938 they were approaching Kaifeng across the North China Plain. China's leader at the time, Chiang Kai Shek, ordered the dykes to be blown up to halt

the Japanese advance. Water surged out of the breach engulfing not only the enemy but also towns, villages and farms. Thousands of people drowned and crops in vast areas of northern China were destroyed. The river's course switched hundreds of kilometres from north to south.

It is estimated that in total about 890,000 people died and 2.5 million were made homeless from that disaster. It took another twenty years to drain the swamps that had formed and to irrigate and reclaim the devastated areas. The river was diverted back to its original channel (now its present course) in 1947 with the help of an international team of engineers.

Today a pumping station takes water from the river to the fields at the point where the Yellow River dykes were blown up in 1938. The writing on the stone dykes says, 'Bring the Yellow River under control!'

9. CONTROLLING THE YELLOW DRAGON

Problems of control

About four thousand years ago, Yu the Great, the legendary controller of floods, is supposed to have said, 'Whoever controls the Yellow River controls China.' Various dynasties have succeeded in partly taming this unpredictable river but two things make it difficult: the area's irregular rainfall and the vast amount of silt that the river carries.

Most of the rain in the Yellow River basin falls during the four summer months, so there is a big change in the level during the year, the river rising to its highest point in summer. In addition, because the rain often falls in torrents, the river can rise very suddenly. Not only can this cause the river to flood, but also the power of the sudden streams erodes the landscape very quickly, adding to the silt in the river.

Few rivers in the world carry as much silt as the Yellow River – it contains seventeen times more than the Nile, for example. Every year so much silt is brought downstream that a dyke 1 metre high and 1 metre wide could be built which would circle the Equator twenty-seven times! About half the silt is dropped on its way downriver, mostly on the North China Plain, and the rest is carried on to the sea.

This irrigation canal in Ningxia is full of muddy water. The Yellow River brings tonnes of silt downstream every year.

Old methods of control

Millions of people have laboured by hand for hundreds of years in the struggle to tame the Yellow River. Most of the works that were carried out were designed to prevent flooding, although some had irrigation and navigation uses. The main method of control was to build, strengthen, extend or raise the height of existing dykes.

However, dyke building is not always a good solution. Containing the river by this method means that it will continue to dump silt between the dykes, thus raising its bed higher and higher above the surrounding plain. If the dykes break the disaster is much worse because the higher the water rises above the plain the greater its force as it pours out.

The motto has therefore been, 'Keep low the dykes, keep deep the channels.' The Chinese realized this early on and, as well as strengthening the dykes, they found dredging the channels to remove silt proved very effective.

In many ways, the methods of controlling the Yellow River have changed very little over the centuries. Since the Communists came to power, the dykes on both sides of the river have been improved to make banks between 10 and 20 metres wide along about 800 kilometres of the river's lower course. They have been strengthened too by building stone walls and piers. Smaller dykes have also been built along the river's tributaries. Dredging is regularly undertaken and the sediment dug out is used to strengthen the dykes.

Dyke building is carried out by hand in many places, as it has been for thousands of years.

Deepening the bed of the Yellow River today – a man with a hose loosens the silt, which is then pumped out on to the surrounding countryside.

Modern developments

These traditional methods are not the only way the river is controlled today. The Chinese have a saying, 'walking on two legs', which refers to combining age-old Chinese ways of doing things, such as building dykes and dredging the river, with modern western ways, such as building dams.

In the 1950s the Communists decided that controlling the Yellow River was a priority. After many surveys and reports, made with help from the then Soviet Union, a plan was drawn up with several purposes: to control flooding, to provide irrigation water, to use the river to generate power and to make the river navigable. Called the Staircase Plan, the idea was to build a series of forty-six dams on the main river, each level being a sort of step up the river. The dams would control the irregular flow of water by storing flood water in the reservoirs, and the reservoirs could regularly supply irrigation channels with water where and when it was needed.

Although this plan was not followed completely, nine large dams and several hundred smaller ones have been constructed along the Yellow River and its tributaries. As well as regulating the water flow, many of these are designed to produce hydroelectric power or to improve irrigation. Developing hydroelectricity wherever possible is important in China because much of the country is short of energy supplies.

Sanmenxia Dam, built across the Yellow River to control flooding and provide electricity.

Sanmenxia

The biggest of the dams was built at Sanmenxia (which means 'Three Gate Gorge' in Chinese). It appeared to be a good place to build a dam because 90 per cent of the river's drainage area was upstream of the dam. However, between half and 1 million people had to be resettled and the dam failed to do its job. The amount of sediment brought down by the river was greatly underestimated and after the dam's completion in 1960, silt quickly began to fill the reservoir and threaten the areas upstream with flooding. In addition, the hydroelectric turbines could not cope with so much silt.

The dam had to be substantially rebuilt to let more water and silt through. Tunnels were constructed round the main dam to allow water out and special turbines were fitted which were resistant to damage from the silt. Afterwards the dam was only able to produce one-fifth of the original hydroelectric power that had been hoped for. It was also not as useful for flood control as expected: the summer flood waters carry more than 80 per cent of the annual silt load and so, in order to stop excessive silting, much of this water has to be let through, with the possibility of flooding downstream.

Just upstream of Sanmenxia, another large dam called Xiaolangdi is due to be built which, it is hoped, will be more effective for flood control. However, since 1949 the Chinese government has achieved a major aim: to have no major floods from the Yellow River. The dam at Sanmenxia has certainly reduced the flood risk. However, recent developments in flood control would never have succeeded in taming the Yellow River over the last forty years without the continuing use of the old methods such as dyke building and dredging.

Other controls

Another method used in flood control is to redirect water during the flood season into storage lakes. One such lake is Dongping, which lies close to the Yellow River on the North China Plain. Excess water from the river is channelled through sluice gates into the lake, which also provides a reservoir for irrigation.

The problems due to unreliable rainfall can generally be dealt with by water storage and irrigation. However, a permanent solution has yet to be found for the vast quantity of silt which clogs up dams and is deposited on the river bed when it reaches the plain. As well as dredging the river bed, a temporary answer is to create 'silt-settling' ponds. Water is pumped or fed into areas beside the river where the silt falls to the bottom. The clear water can then be used for irrigation or returned to the river.

The water behind Qingtongxia Dam in Ningxia is thick with muddy silt.

Erosion control

The only effective way to halt the silt is to control the erosion of the loess which is the source of the silt. Before 200 BC, the loess plateau was largely unfarmed and wooded. At that time the Yellow River's silt content was about 50 per cent of what it is today – the river was known as the Great River, not the Yellow River. As the Chinese empire expanded trees were cut down, hills were ploughed and erosion began in earnest. Nowadays across the loess area, about 1 cm of topsoil is lost every year.

There are several schemes to control the erosion. Terracing of fields can prevent rain-water running off the land, taking the soil with it. The landscape today in some areas of Shaanxi and Shanxi provinces is an endless sea of hills with terraces cut to follow the contours. However, many slopes are still unterraced and few farmers can afford

A farmer works on an irrigation canal supplying vital water to the fields.

Trees are planted in the frail loess soil to try to halt erosion.

machines to help them or spare the time to do the hard work that is involved to create new terraces.

Afforestation, or planting trees, is the most effective way to stop the erosion because the tree roots help to hold the soil in place. In 1977 a massive tree-planting project was begun, with over 6 million people working to dig in trees on the steep loess. Unfortunately, the trees were not tended properly afterwards and in the dry climate many died from lack of water. Tree planting is still encouraged, but it needs a great deal of effort and care to be successful.

Another method is to build soil retention dams. Small dams are built across valleys and gullies and these prevent the soil from being washed out of the valley. If the surrounding slopes are then grassed or forested, by the time the dam fills (perhaps between fifteen to twenty years later), the land around it should be stabilized.

A floating bridge across the Yellow River at Jinan lies on the dry bed of the river. All its water has been taken for irrigation or diverted upstream.

Water needs

There is a new problem for the future facing those who control the Yellow River: water shortages. The expanding population and new industrial developments have led to a massive increase in the use of and demand for water. New irrigation channels, hundreds of kilometres long, feed dry, uncultivated areas which are being converted to farmland. Industry is expanding faster than ever before in China and water is needed in many of the industrial processes. In cities such as the capital, Beijing, water consumption has doubled because the people now have modern conveniences, such as washing machines and showers.

At certain times of the year, when the rainfall is low, so much water is taken off for irrigation and industry that at places on the North China Plain, such as Jinan,

the river runs dry. More water can be let out of dams higher up, but this reduces their ability to produce hydroelectricity.

The whole of north China is finding itself short of water. In an attempt to solve the problem, plans have been announced to divert water from southern China, where rainfall is high, to northern China. The idea would be to bring water from the Yangzi River which has twenty times more water than the Yellow River. It is suggested that the old route of the Grand Canal could be used to divert the water for more than a thousand kilometres to the north.

China has survived many disasters in the past. Today, by combining modern technology with age-old solutions and the vast numbers of people who are available to work, the government is determined to control this great river and use it for the benefit of China's fast-growing population and economy.

45

GLOSSARY

Altitude   The height of land above sea level.

Archaeologists   People who study the past.

Barbarians   Primitive or uncivilized people.

Basin   The land drained by a river and its tributaries.

Bauxite   A clay which contains the metal aluminium.

Buddhism   A religion based on the teachings of the ancient Indian prophet, Buddha.

Delta   A flat, fan-shaped area of land at the mouth of a river which reaches the sea in two or more branches.

Drainage area   The area the river drains.

Dredging   Deepening a river by digging out its bed.

Drought   A long period with no rain.

Dyke   An earth bank usually beside a river; sometimes called a levee.

Dynasties   Long lines of rulers who come from the same family.

Erosion   The wearing away of rocks by the action of water, ice, wind, etc.

Extinct   Describing a kind of animal or plant no longer found alive.

Fertile   Able to produce good crops.

Hydroelectricity   Electricity produced by the pressure of falling water.

Industrialization   The development of industry on a large scale.

Irrigate   To carry water to the land using canals.

Kaoliang   A kind of grain – it is also called sorghum. It is coarser than wheat but withstands drought. Its strong stalk has been used in dyke building.

Loess   A light-coloured fine-grained deposit of particles of earth, blown and deposited by the wind.

Minority groups   Groups that are different from a larger group of which they are a part.

Mosques   Places where Muslims pray.

Muslims   Followers of Islam, the religion founded by the Prophet Muhammad.

Navigable   Describes a waterway that is wide, deep and safe enough for boats.

Nomads   People who do not live in a fixed place but move around.

Noodles   Strips of dough, eaten in soup or served with a sauce.

Persecution   Causing suffering to people, especially because of their religious beliefs.

Pilgrimages   Journeys to sacred or religious places.

Plateau   A large area of high and fairly flat land.

Private enterprise   Economic activity carried out by private individuals or organizations that are privately owned.

Reaches   Stretches of a river.

Refinery   A factory where natural resources such as oil are treated and purified.

Reservoirs   Human-made lakes in which water is stored.

Sediment   Material such as mud, sand or stone carried by a river.

Silt   Very fine particles carried by a river.

Silk Road   An ancient overland route used by traders to carry silk and other goods between China and countries in the West.

Socialist state   A system in which the state (the people of a country under a government) runs the country's wealth.

Smelt   To separate metal from other material by heating it.

Stabilize   To make firm.

Terraces   Raised level banks of earth, like big steps, on the side of a hill.

Tributaries   Rivers that run into other larger ones.

Turbines   Motors that are turned by water or wind and produce electricity.

Yak   A kind of ox with a thick coat that keeps it warm in freezing weather; it only survives at high altitudes.

READING LIST

China by Philip Steele (Macmillan, 1989)
Countries of the World: China by Julia Waterlow (Wayland, 1989)
Focus on China by Jessie Lim (Evans Bros, 1991)
Yellow River by K. J. Gregory (Wayland, 1980)

For older readers:
China: a Geographical Survey by T. R. Tregear (Hodder & Stoughton, 1980)
China by Philip Steele (Macmillan, 1989)

China's Sorrow by Lynn Pan (Century Publishing, 1985)
China's Sorrow The Geographical Magazine (February 1988)
China: the Land and the People by D. C. Money (Evans Bros, 1990)
China Today by D. C. Money (Cambridge University Press, 1987)
Focus on China by Jessie Lim (Evans Bros, 1991)
Yellow River by Kevin Sinclair (Weidenfeld and Nicolson, 1987)

ADDRESSES

Great Britain-China Centre
15 Belgrave Square
London SW1X 8PS

Cultural Section
Chinese Embassy
11 West Heath Road
London NW3

The Society for Anglo-Chinese
  Understanding
109 Promenade
Cheltenham
Gloucester GL50 1NW

The following places have interesting Chinese collections:

Victoria and Albert Museum
Cromwell Road
London

Manchester Chinese Arts Centre
36 Charlotte Street
Manchester M1 4FD

To help you pronounce some of the Chinese words in this book, look at the following guide:
zh is pronounced *j*   *x* is pronounced *sh*   *q* is pronounced *ch*

Picture acknowledgements
All photographs including the cover are by Julia Waterlow. The map on page 5 is by Peter Bull Design. Artwork on pages 8, 10, 37 is by John Yates.

INDEX